Caring

By Bruce S. Glassman

With an Introduction by
Michael Josephson,
Founder of CHARACTER COUNTS!SM

JOSEPHSON
INSTITUTE
CHARACTERCOUNTS!

Produced and created in partnership with Josephson Institute

Special Thanks goes to the following people, whose help on this project was invaluable:

At CHARACTER COUNTS!:
Michael Josephson
Rich Jarc
Amanda Skinner
Mimi Drop
Michelle Del Castillo

Content Advisers:
Dave Bender, book publisher
Tracy Hughes, educator
& CHARACTER COUNTS!
coordinator for Meadowbrook
Middle School, San Diego
Cindy De Clercq, Elementary
School Principal

And thanks to:
Nathan Glassman-Hughes,
Emma Glassman-Hughes,
Natalia Mata, Erica Warren,
Ebony Sanders, Kellen
O'Connell, Nicole Rigler,
and Alex Olberding

Library of Congress Cataloging-in-Publication Data

Glassman, Bruce.
Caring / written by Bruce S. Glassman. — 1st ed.
p. cm. — (Six Pillars of Character series)
Includes bibliographical references and index.
ISBN-13: 978-1-60108-500-9 (hardcover); ISBN-10: 1-60108-500-1 (hardcover)
ISBN-13: 978-1-60108-501-6 (pbk.); ISBN-10: 1-60108-501-X (pbk.)
1. Caring—Juvenile literature. I. Title.

BJ1475.G53 2009
177.7—dc22   2008001182
Printed in China

Contents

Thinking About Character

By Michael Josephson, Founder, CHARACTER COUNTS!

Imagine that you're taking a big test at the end of the year. You really want to do well on it. You're stuck on a few questions—answers you know will make the difference between a good grade and a possible poor grade. You look up from your test and realize that you can clearly read the answers from the student sitting next to you. You're now faced with a choice. Do you copy the answers or do you go back to staring at your own sheet?

You consider the choices. You know that, if you cheat, you probably won't get caught. And, you think to yourself, copying a few answers is relatively harmless. Who does it hurt? And, besides, everyone does it, right?

Every day you are faced with choices that test your character.

So, what do you do?

Your honest answer to this question will tell you a great deal about your character. Your answer reflects not only what you know is right and wrong, but also how you *act* with what you know.

You are faced with important choices every day. Some choices are "preference choices"—for example, what to wear to school, what to buy for lunch, or what to buy your dad for his birthday. Other choices are "ethical choices." These choices are about what's right and wrong. These are the choices that reflect character.

Ethics play a part in more daily decisions than you may think. The test-taking scenario is only one example of an ethical choice.

You are faced with ethical choices every day. One of the main goals of this series is to show you how to recognize which choices are ethical choices. Another main goal is to show you how to make the right ethical choices.

About Being Ethical

Being ethical isn't simply about what is allowed—or legal—and what is not. You can often find a legal way to do what is unethical. Maybe you saw that a cashier at the grocery store forgot to ring up one of your items. There is no law that says you must tell him or her. But, is it ethical to just walk out without mentioning it? The answer is no. You're still being dishonest by taking something you did not pay for.

So, being ethical is about something more than "what you can get away with." It is about what you do because *you know it's the right thing to do*—regardless of who's watching and regardless of whether you may stand to gain. Often there is a price to pay for doing the right thing.

Character Takes Courage

There are many obstacles to being ethical—chances are you're faced with some of them every day. Maybe you don't want to be

There are many obstacles to being ethical. Overcoming them takes courage and hard work.

embarrassed by telling the truth. Or maybe you feel doing the right thing will take too much effort. Few good things come without a cost. Becoming a person of character is hard work. Here is a poem I wrote that makes this point.

It's Not Easy

Let's be honest. Ethics is not for wimps.

It's not easy being a good person.

It's not easy to be honest when it might be costly, to play fair when others cheat or to keep inconvenient promises.

It's not easy to stand up for our beliefs and still respect differing viewpoints.

It's not easy to control powerful impulses, to be accountable for our attitudes and actions, to tackle unpleasant tasks or to sacrifice the now for later.

It's not easy to bear criticism and learn from it without getting angry, to take advice or to admit error.

It's not easy to really feel genuine remorse and apologize sincerely, or to accept an apology graciously and truly forgive.

It's not easy to stop feeling like a victim, to resist cynicism and to make the best of every situation.

It's not easy to be consistently kind, to think of others first, to judge generously, to give the benefit of the doubt.

It's not easy to be grateful or to give without concern for reward or gratitude.

It's not easy to fail and still keep trying, to learn from failure, to risk failing again, to start over, to lose with grace or to be glad for the success of another.

It's not easy to avoid excuses and rationalizations or to resist temptations.

No, being a person of character is not easy.

That's why it's such a lofty goal and an admirable achievement.

Character Is Worth It!

I sincerely hope that you will learn and use the ideas of CHARACTER COUNTS! The books in this series will show you the core values (the Six Pillars) of good character. These values will help you in all aspects of your life—and for many years to come. I encourage you to use these ideas as a kind of "guide-rail" on your journey to adulthood. With "guide-rails," your journey is more likely to bring you to a place where you can be a truly good, happy, and ethical person.

Michael Josephson
Founder of Josephson Institute and CHARACTER COUNTS!

chapter 1

What Is Caring?

When you hear the word *caring,* you probably think of things you care about. For example, you care about your family and pets. You may care about getting good grades in school. You may care about winning your next soccer game. We all recognize these kinds of caring as part of our daily lives.

The kind of caring that comes with good character is a "bigger" kind of caring. It requires compassion (feeling) and kindness toward others. It also requires generosity, charity, and sharing. Most importantly, this caring is not only for those you know and love, but toward all others—maybe complete strangers.

Caring requires compassion, kindness, and generosity toward others.

During times of crisis, we often see the most dramatic examples of caring. After Hurricane Katrina devastated the Gulf Coast in August 2005, tens of thousands of people from all over the world reached out to help. Many of those people lived far away from the disaster. In some cases, volunteers drove for thousands of miles to be in Louisiana or Mississippi to help victims. Those people showed extraordinary kindness and compassion.

When wildfires destroyed nearly 2,000 homes and hundreds of thousands of acres throughout Southern California in October 2007, residents and non-residents alike came together in a spirit of caring. The fires raged for more than a week. Nearly half a million people had their lives turned upside down. Almost immediately, shelters and evacuation centers were up and running, and donations of food and clothing poured in. This was all a result of people showing great compassion and kindness for others during a time of crisis.

New Orleans residents walk the flooded streets after Hurricane Katrina.

Caring is not only about being kind or generous during times of crisis. It's also about being that way every day. For caring to truly be part of your character, it needs to be one of the priorities in your life. We'll talk more about this in Chapter 3.

In 2007, thousands of homes were destroyed by wildfires in Southern California.

Two Parts to Caring

Caring as it relates to character is shown in two basic ways:

1. as concern for others
2. as a passion for an ideal, belief, or cause.

Most often, these two ways go together. A person who shows a constant concern for others most likely believes passionately in the idea of helping others. A truly caring person is involved in the well-being of others, as if their own happiness depended on it.

Concern for Others: Compassion and Empathy

Compassion and *empathy* are words that are often used to describe a true concern for others. Compassion means being affected by the suffering of others and feeling the urge to help. Empathy is the ability

Caring people are affected emotionally by the suffering of others.

to share and "identify with" another person's thoughts and feelings. A truly caring person is emotionally affected by the pain or pleasure of others.

Concern for Others: Charity

Charity is about giving of yourself for the benefit of others. Charity can come in any shape or size. It can be a small donation of money or a large one. It can be a gift of time, support, comfort, or goods. The important part of charity is that it is done solely for the sake of someone else—and not for anything in return. Many charitable actions go along with some sort of sacrifice. A sacrifice is when the person who is giving does without something important. That something can be money, time, goods, etc.

It is also important to remember that the size of a donation or charitable gift does not mirror the size of the sacrifice in giving it. For example, consider this:

A local charity received two donations at the same time: one was a $10,000 donation made by a billionaire businessman and the other was a $1 donation that came from a homeless man.

Who do you think made the bigger sacrifice? Do you think the money given was more important to the billionaire or to the homeless man?

So, even small acts of caring are "big" if they require a big sacrifice.

Concern for Others: Mercy and Forgiveness

Extending forgiveness to others is part of being truly caring. To forgive someone for a wrong, a caring person must try to understand why the wrong happened. The next step is to accept it and "move on." Moving on means you are no longer bothered by the wrong.

Mercy is about being generous with your forgiveness. It means doing your best to let another person move on after a wrong.

Charity is a selfless act meant to help others.

Having mercy is also known as giving someone "a break" or "cutting them some slack." Sometimes it means being willing to offer a second chance. Consider this story about mercy and forgiveness:

Todd and Mark had been best friends all through elementary school. In middle school, they met new people and had other friends as well. In sixth grade, Mark became really good friends with Skylar. Just about this time, people told Mark that personal, private information and nasty rumors were being spread around school about him. When Mark found out that it was Todd who was spreading the rumors, he became very angry. He refused to speak to Todd, or even look at him as they passed in the hallway.

Two weeks later, Todd caught up to Mark in the hallway and asked to talk to him. Mark didn't want to, but he found it hard to refuse his oldest friend. Todd explained that what he had done was wrong and that he was sorry. He admitted that he was very jealous of Mark's new friend. He started the rumors out of spite and because he was hurt. He realized now that he made a big mistake.

Mark was still very angry about the whole thing.

But, he dug down deep inside himself. Now that he knew the whole story, he decided to give Todd another chance. He decided to forgive him. He decided to put the problem behind them and to move on. From that day forward—thanks to Mark's forgiveness—Todd, Mark, and Skylar became inseparable.

Mark showed his friend mercy and forgiveness. He not only gave his friend a chance to explain and apologize, Mark also decided to forgive and move on. Can you think of a time when you could have been more forgiving? Or a time when you wish someone had been more forgiving toward you?

Concern for Others: Kindness and Consideration

On a more personal level, these two parts of caring are about how you interact with others. Kindness and consideration mean being understanding and open-minded. They also mean being respectful of others. When you are kind and considerate to everyone—regardless of who they are—you are being truly caring.

Consider how you think about and treat others. Do you treat your parents and grandparents with respect? Do you show the same respect to other adults? Are you kind and respectful with your siblings and your friends? Do you show kindness to people you don't know—a new neighbor, an elderly woman at the supermarket, a person asking for money on the sidewalk?

Caring As Passion for a Belief or Cause

Having a passion for an important belief or cause is a big part of good character. It means you are able to care about things other than yourself. Being selfless and giving is a big part of being a good citizen of the world.

The first part of caring—which we already discussed—focuses mostly on how you act toward other individuals in your life. This second part of caring has a lot to do with concern for others, too. But this part of caring is about "big ideas" that affect many people. This part of caring is about ideals—the way you wish something should

Your actions reflect your passion for a belief or cause that you feel is important.

be. For example, you may care about the environment. As part of a passion for that cause, you may volunteer your time to help organize a recycling program at your school. You may do other things in your life that reflect your passion. For example, you may take extra care not to waste food or water. All these actions would reflect your caring about an ideal—the ideal of protecting the planet and not being wasteful with its resources.

The Elements of Passion

Passion usually has four elements, or parts:

1. Conviction   3. Persistence
2. Commitment   4. Endurance

Conviction: This is a strong belief that an idea or ideal is right—such as protecting the environment. Convictions can also be very personal things. Often, people have opposing convictions. For example, some people believe strongly that it should be the government's job to provide health insurance to every citizen. Other people believe—just as strongly—that health insurance should be the responsibility of individuals. There is no single right answer.

Commitment: When you show a true passion for something—when you truly care—you are committed to it regardless of the consequences. If, for example, you are committed to protecting the environment, you won't buy things that are packaged in wasteful packaging or made from materials that are not recycled—even if they are much less expensive. Commitment

Your commitment is reflected in all the choices you make.

means you are willing to "pay the price" of your convictions. For example, people who protested for civil rights in the 1960s often staged marches and "sit-ins" to demand change. The protestors knew that they would likely be arrested for their actions—maybe even beaten—but they protested anyway. They had the strength of their convictions and a commitment to their cause. And they knew their cause was just. (**Remember:** Believing strongly that your cause is right does not mean your action is justified. Many people who have had strong convictions have done things that are not right. Strength of your convictions and your willingness to accept consequences can only be if your actions do not hurt anyone else.)

Sometimes, your dedication to an idea will be "inconvenient" or will cause discomfort. For example, if your organization is marching to support a recycling bill on Sunday morning, you may have to get up extra early to take part. Or you may have to cancel plans with a friend. If you are truly committed, you will accept the negative along with the positive.

Persistence: This is really about attitude. *Persistent* means being determined to not give up. For example, the first time you try to get other students involved in a school recycling program, you might be turned down by everyone. If you're persistent, you won't stop trying even if you fail the first time. You will keep talking to people about your cause until you've convinced enough of them to help.

Endurance: Persistence is about attitude, but endurance is really about action. It means lasting long enough to have an effect, despite tough obstacles. It means, for example, when you get the recycling program ready to go, you make sure it stays running long enough to truly make a difference.

Caring Is the "Heart" of Ethics

Caring is the element that allows people of character to balance all the Six Pillars properly. It reminds us to keep the well-being of others in mind with all we do. As we have discussed, nothing is good if it is done to excess. Caring shows us how to put the Six Pillars of Character into use for the best positive effect.

For example, caring helps to:

• **Balance Trustworthiness:** we want to be honest, but not so blunt that we hurt someone else.

Being persistent means not giving up on what you believe.

- **Balance Respect:** by respecting other people's right to make their own choices, but not choices that hurt themselves or others.
- **Balance Responsibility:** by being accountable for ourselves, but not ONLY to ourselves.
- **Balance Fairness:** by providing just punishment, but not without appropriate mercy and forgiveness.
- **Balance Citizenship:** by being a good member of the world at large, but also being a good member of your family.

Princess Diana

When Diana Spencer married Prince Charles in 1981, she became the Princess of Wales. From the moment she stepped into the spotlight, Diana captured the hearts of millions all over the world. She was shy and humble. She came from one of England's most distinguished families, but she seemed like a "regular" person. What struck people most, was Diana's genuine sweetness and her sense of caring and compassion.

Princess Diana felt great compassion for the sick.

Diana soon became well known for her support of many different charities. Part of this was her role as Princess of Wales—for example, she was expected to make hospital visits to comfort the sick. In terms of caring, Diana went beyond what was simply expected of her. For example, she used her celebrity and influence to work for a campaign against landmines, a cause that won the Nobel Peace Prize in 1997. She also worked to reduce discrimination against victims of AIDS.

A Champion of AIDS Awareness

In April 1987, Princess Diana was one of the first high-profile celebrities to be photographed touching a person infected with HIV. Her public display of compassion raised awareness and understanding around the world. Diana's action was simple, but it was brave. The effect of her appearances was to change world opinion of AIDS sufferers. In December 2001, former U.S. President Bill Clinton said:

> In 1987, when so many still believed that AIDS could be contracted through casual contact, Princess Diana sat on the sickbed of a man with AIDS and held his hand. She showed the world that people with AIDS deserve no isolation, but compassion and kindness. It helped change the world's opinion, and gave hope to those with AIDS.

Diana also made many private visits to show kindness to the sick. According to London nurses who saw her, Diana would often turn up unannounced at hospices and hospitals. And she would always have specific instructions that her visit be kept a secret from the media.

Raising Awareness About Landmines

In the 1990s, Diana worked to raise awareness about landmines that were injuring and killing innocent children all over the world. While touring an Angolan minefield, Diana was photographed in a helmet and flak jacket. The image became an instant news item and raised awareness worldwide.

On August 31, 1997, Diana died in a car accident in Paris, France. She was only 36 years old. Though her life was tragically short, Diana left a legacy of compassion and caring that is still remembered to this day.

The Importance of Caring

T hroughout our history, caring and compassion have truly changed the world. Over the centuries, people who have shown outstanding compassion have influenced us in two ways: they have made good change happen, but they have also inspired a passion in others to be caring.

Caring and Spirituality

The ideals of caring and compassion form a good deal of many faiths. And many notable religious leaders throughout history have made

In 1985, a huge charity rock concert in Philadelphia raised millions for famine relief in Africa.

compassion a central part of their message. The Jewish Torah, Jesus Christ, Buddha, and Muhammad, for example, focused much of their messages on compassion, caring, and love. Most major religions have compassion as a centerpiece of their belief systems.

People Who Have Made a Difference

So many individuals have made a difference with their passion for a cause. They have been people of all faiths, from all cultures, from all ethnic backgrounds, and from all eras. Because so many have made a difference, it is difficult to single out only one or two. Here is a brief look at a few individuals whose caring and compassion for human beings left a powerful legacy.

Jane Addams

In 1860, Jane Addams was born into a wealthy family in Illinois. While traveling in Europe as a young woman, she saw a lot of human suffering. After witnessing the terrible living conditions in a London slum, Jane realized she had found her passion.

Jane Addams

Jane and her friend Ellen Gates Starr founded Hull House in 1889. Set in a poor section of Chicago, Hull House was the first "settlement

Caring at the Center of Faith

Following is just one message about caring (of many) from some of the world's major religions.

Buddhism: "As a mother with her own life guards the life of her own child, let those all-embracing thoughts for all that lives be thine."

Islam: "Be kind to parents, and the near kinsman, and to orphans, and to the needy, and to the neighbor who is of kin, and to the neighbor who is a stranger, and to the companion at your side, and to the traveler."

Judaism: "Thou shalt love thy neighbor as thyself."

Confucianism: "He who's heart is in the smallest degree set upon Goodness will dislike no one."

Jainism: "Have benevolence towards all living beings, joy at the sight of the virtuous, compassion and sympathy for the afflicted, and tolerance toward the indolent and ill-behaved."

Christianity: "A new commandment I give to you. That ye love one another; even as I have loved you, that ye also love one another. By this all men will know that ye are my disciples, if ye have love one to another."

Baha'i: "Be kind to all people, love humanity, consider all mankind as your relations and servants of the most high God."

Sikhism: "No one shall cause another pain or injury; All mankind shall live in peace together."

house" in America. Its goal was to help Chicago's poorest people. Walking among the neighborhoods, Jane saw the need to change laws that affected the lives of the poor. She worked fiercely to improve safety for workers in factories. She also worked to improve working hours for women and children.

Her compassion and perseverance kept Jane going for many decades. Later in her life, she became a founder of the American Civil Liberties Union (ACLU). The ACLU worked to defend human and legal rights for everyone regardless of class, gender, or race. She was also one of the founders of the National Association for the Advancement of Colored People (NAACP). The NAACP worked to improve the lives of African Americans.

In 1931, Jane Addams became the first American woman to be awarded the Nobel Peace Prize. The honor was in recognition of a lifetime dedicated to caring, compassion, and a true desire to help improve the lives of people who could not help themselves.

Marian Wright Edelman

Born in 1939, Marian Wright grew up in Bennetsville, South Carolina. After graduating from college in 1960, Marian got a law degree from Yale University.

Marian wanted to use her law degree in ways that would help poor and disadvantaged people. In 1973, she founded the

Children's Defense Fund (CDF). The CDF was devoted to helping children's causes in America. As the CDF's chief spokesperson, Marian persuaded Congress to improve America's foster care system. She also worked to improve standards for child care. She lobbied to improve protections for children with disabilities, and also for children who are homeless, abused, or neglected.

Marian has been honored with many awards for her work. She has received the Albert

Marian Wright Edelman is one of America's leaders for children's causes.

Schweitzer Humanitarian Prize, as well as the 2000 Presidential Medal of Freedom.

Today, the CDF continues to be one of America's most influential organizations for the protection of children. Marian believes strongly that everyone has a responsibility to improve the world and to better the lives of others. As she said, "If you don't like the way the world is, you have an obligation to change it. Just do it one step at a time."

Bono

Bono is the lead singer for the superstar rock band U2. His face and his music are known to millions of people all over the world. Bono has used his celebrity to help others.

Since 1986, Bono has been active in many charities and organizations that work to improve the health of poor people in poor nations. Much of Bono's work has focused on Africa. He has traveled the world, speaking to leaders in many countries and at the United Nations. He has helped to create a number of programs—such as (RED) clothing-- that work to stop the spread of AIDS in Africa. He has helped to provide economic help to Africa's poorest areas. Bono has also been a very active member of Amnesty International, which works to protect human rights around the world.

Bono's passion for helping others has been recognized by many. He has been honored with a Liberty Medal in Philadelphia, and was nominated for a Nobel Peace Prize in 2006. On various occasions, Nelson Mandela, the President of the United States,

Bono has been honored by many for his caring.

the Prime Minister of Britain, and the head of the United Nations have publicly praised Bono's commitment and passion. They have thanked him for being a shining example of caring to people all over the world.

Oprah Winfrey

As one of the world's most famous and successful people, Oprah Winfrey has a lot of power. In 2003, she became the first African-American woman in history to become a billionaire. Luckily, she has chosen to use her influence and resources to make a positive difference in the world.

Oprah's great success started when she became television's most popular talk-show host. But it didn't end there. Oprah went on to become a highly successful producer and an actress. Her production company—Harpo Films—has produced many television and theatrical productions.

Even though Oprah is part of so many different projects and programs, she remains dedicated to expanding her charity work. Over the years, Oprah has created numerous programs and organizations to help others.

In 1997, Oprah hosted an episode of her talk show that encouraged viewers to make a difference in the lives of others. On that show, Oprah spoke to her audience: "I want you to open your hearts and see the world in a different way. You get from the world what you give to the world. I promise this will change your life for the better."

That episode led to the creation of a public charity called Oprah's Angel Network, which collects donations from Oprah's audiences and fans. To date, this charity has raised more than $50 million. The money has gone to establish scholarships and schools for underprivileged kids, to support women's shelters, and to build youth centers and homes in poor areas.

In 2002, The Oprah Winfrey Foundation expanded its efforts to South Africa. There, the foundation created a program to help orphanages and poor schools. Oprah said, while visiting the orphanages, that she "...Realized in those moments why I was born, why I am not married, and why I do not have children of my own. These are my children. I made a decision to be a voice for those children, to empower them, to help educate them, so the spirit that burns alive inside each of them does not die." All in all, 50,000 children received gifts of food, clothing, and school supplies. Sixty-three schools received libraries and teacher education.

During one of her visits to South Africa, Oprah made a promise to a very important man. The man was Nelson Mandela. And the promise was that Oprah would help to build a school in South Africa. To accomplish this, the Oprah Winfrey Leadership Academy Foundation was created. Oprah personally donated more than $40 million to this

Oprah Winfrey opens her leadership school in South Africa.

effort. In 2007, the school in South Africa finally opened and took in its first class of girls.

Oprah's compassion and commitment to helping people has not gone unnoticed. She has been honored by many organizations over the years. The Elie Wiesel Foundation for Humanity gave her its Humanitarian Award in 2007. Other awards include the 2005 National Freedom Award from the National Civil Rights Museum, and the Global Humanitarian Action Award from the United Nations. Oprah has also been listed as one of *Time* magazine's "100 Most Influential People in the World" more than five times.

chapter **3**

Caring in Your Life

You have read a lot in the previous chapters about people who have done wonderful things for the world. Many of their accomplishments took a lifetime to achieve. Not all acts of caring, however, need to be done on such a large scale. There are many ways that you can make caring, compassion, and charity a part of your life today.

Caring comes in all sizes. And not all caring is the same. The love and commitment you show your immediate family is not always the same as the compassion you show to your friends. And the personal caring you show is different from the "bigger" caring you may do by working for a cause that helps people you don't even know.

Caring about the environment is one kind of "bigger" caring.

Your Caring Can Make a Difference Now

One of the most important things to remember is that all acts of caring make a difference. Some differences are small, others are large. Don't assume that the "small things" won't make a difference. Or that they are not "worth" doing. They are all worth doing—and each act of true kindness and compassion helps others as it helps you become a better human being. A person of true character incorporates caring into daily life as much as possible.

The Two Parts of Caring

Your concern for others will be shown in the ways you act with your family, friends, and those you see every day. If you have true character, you will show everyone compassion, empathy, kindness, and consideration—even if you have never met them before. If it is necessary, you will also show others charity, mercy, and forgiveness.

Do you care about endangered animals?

Think for a moment about your daily life. Is there a way to add an act of kindness or compassion to your life tomorrow? Maybe there's a new student in your school who just transferred mid-year and doesn't know anyone. Or maybe someone you know has been sick or lost a loved one.

Suitcases for Kids

When Aubyn Burnside was 11 years old, she heard about foster care. She learned that most children in foster care programs had to carry their belongings around in garbage bags because they could not afford suitcases. Knowing this saddened Aubyn. "I thought they must feel like garbage themselves," she said. Aubyn was saddened, but she was also inspired to do something. So, together with her brother Welland, she founded Suitcases for Kids, an organization that supplies children in foster care with a suitcase of their own.

In January 1995, Aubyn started out by making posters and speeches in her community of Hickory, North Carolina. "I expected to start seeing some donations of suitcases," she recalls. "I figured people would be getting new luggage as Christmas gifts, and in turn would get rid of their old luggage." For a while she received nothing.

Aubyn was persistent and determined. She and Welland took a trip to the Salvation Army. There, they bought 31 suitcases for $15. Those suitcases helped to get her effort going. Soon, other donations poured in.

By the end of 1996, the Burnsides had personally collected over 25,000 suitcases. Today, hundreds of thousands are collected annually. SFK is active in all 50 states and in 87 foreign countries.

Whatever the circumstance, thinking about ways to become more caring will strengthen your character enormously.

Do you already have causes or beliefs that you are passionate about? You are never too young (or too old) to have a passion. What are the things that stir your passion? The environment? Endangered animals? The homeless?

Things You Can Do (Don't Wait for the Holidays)

Have you ever noticed that there seems to be a big spike in caring and charity around certain holidays at the end of the year? Holidays are a time when many people talk about charity, giving, and those who are less fortunate. Unfortunately, many people think about these things ONLY during the holidays. The goal of a truly caring person is to live every day as if it's the holiday season. So don't wait for November or December. Here are some thoughts about things you may be able to do anytime (just make sure you ask for the proper permission first):

1. Donate Stuff from Your Room: If you're like most kids, you have a lot of clothes and other things in your room that you no longer want or need. Instead of having them sit around, donate them to an effort where they can be useful to someone else.

2. Use Your Web Site: Have a web site? A Myspace or Facebook page? Talk about your worthy cause(s) and get others to care, too!

3. Donate Your Time: Being caring and passionate is not only about

money. You can donate your time to others as well. There are many ways you can volunteer—for example, you can help out at a nursing home or an animal shelter. You can volunteer to be a tutor, or you can work at the local library or your school library.

4. Convince Your Family and Friends: You and your friends have the power to make a positive difference—especially if you band together. Find a caring project that excites you all and then work on making it happen together. Are there ways you could make your school a better place?

5. Clean up Around Your School or Neighborhood: This is just one example of a simple way you can go out and help your community today. Other ideas may include planting a tree, putting up a birdhouse, or re-painting a worn out fence or sign.

Caring and Choices

Life is all about making choices. Deciding to become a person of good character is a choice. Figuring out to how to be a caring person also involves choices. For example, commitment involves choices: "If I work for this cause, what do I have to give up? My time? Some of my things? Some money?"

Locks of Love

Have you ever thought you're too young to help others? Or that you don't have enough money to make a difference in someone else's life? Consider this:

At St. Timothy Elementary School in Columbus, Ohio, 23 girls donated something they all had plenty of: hair.

As part of the Locks of Love program, the girls grew their hair for a year in order to have it cut and donated to children who permanently lost their hair due to illness, such as cancer. The students ranged in age from fifth graders all the way down to kindergartners.

A Kindergarten student donates her hair at an elementary school in Oklahoma.

The spokesperson for Locks of Love, Lauren Kukkamaa, said, "Children have the most precious, humble, and unselfish hearts of anyone on Earth, and they are just aching to help other children in need." The organization says that 80 percent of all donations come from children who want to help other children.

Charity and forgiveness also involve choices. For example: "Which charities and causes do I work for? When should I forgive? And what should I forgive?"

Learning How to Make Good Choices

A famous lawyer and speechmaker named William Jennings Bryan once said, "Destiny is not a matter of chance, it is a matter of choice." He was saying that we have more control over our lives than we often assume.

More than anything else, your life will be affected by the choices you make. Knowing how to make good choices is most often the difference between being happy and being miserable.

Two Core Principles of Choice-Making

There are two fundamental principles that form the foundation of good decision-making. They are:

1. We all have the power to decide what we do and what we say.
2. We are morally responsible for the consequences of our choices.

The first principle goes back to what William Jennings Bryan said: your destiny is your choice. But what about when you feel powerless and out of control? We all feel this way at times—especially kids and teens.

Seeking good advice from people you trust is key to making sound decisions.

It's important to remember that having the power to make choices doesn't mean you have to make every choice alone. You also have the power to seek out good advice and to get the counsel of people you trust. So, part of making good choices is knowing how to get the help you need to make them.

The second principle is about understanding the full impact of the decisions you make. Every choice has a consequence—whether good or bad. And every choice affects certain people in some way. The people that are affected by a given choice are called "stakeholders." Most of us never even realize how many stakeholders there are for a given choice. Have you ever copied songs from a friend onto your MP3 player? Can you think of all the stakeholders affected by that choice? (Hint: It's not just you and the friend you copied from. Start thinking about the music download service, and the employees at the record company that sells the songs, and the musicians, producers, and engineers that work to create each song...).

So, thinking about all the stakeholders in a decision is one way to consider how important that decision is. It's another way of saying that the greater the consequence of a decision, the more important that decision is.

Okay, so now you know the principles of good decision-making. But the final part of the process is acting—actually making the ethical choice. Most of us know—most of the time—what the ethical choice is. The question is whether we *do it*—even if the consequences are costly to us or to others we care about.

Decision-Making Helpers

Choices are not always clear. Sometimes you will be pulled in many different directions as you consider what to do. Here are a few questions to ask yourself as you consider a decision. The answers may help to make the right choice clearer.

1. **Ask Yourself the Question of Universality**: If everyone made this choice, would it be a good thing?
2. **Ask Yourself the Golden Rule Question**: Would you want someone else to make this choice if it affected you the same way?
3. **Ask Yourself the Role Model Question**: Think of someone you know who is ethical and of strong character. What would that person do?

Building character is a lifelong process that takes courage, persistence, and strength.

Ethics Is Not for Wimps

Remember, being ethical is not always easy. It takes strength. And it often takes courage.

Being a person of strong character is not something that happens in a day or a week, or even years. For most "mere mortals," the strengthening of character is a lifelong process. There are always things to improve. Every year you work at it, your character will get better and better.

Ethical decisions can be difficult to make—and even more difficult to act upon. But great satisfaction and self-esteem come with knowing you did the right thing. Those positive feelings will inspire you to always make the right choices. This kind of satisfaction lasts a lifetime and brings you the most rewarding feeling of all: happiness.

Resources

WEB SITES:

Charactercounts.org: The official site of CHARACTER COUNTS! provides information on programs, offers free resources and materials for students, parents, and teachers; also includes links to many other valuable and related sites.

Justgive.org: Official web site of an organization that works to increase charitable donations by connection people with the causes they care about most.

Wwf.org: Official web site of the World wildlife Fund, which promotes conservation and works to protect endangered animals and habitats.

Locksoflove.org: Official web site of the organization that provides hairpieces to financially disadvantaged children who suffer from long-term hair loss due to illness or any other diagnosis.

Oprahsangelnetwork.org: Web site of one of Oprah Winfrey's charitable foundations. Links will take you to The Oprah Winfrey Foundation and other charitable organizations with which she is affiliated.

NOTABLE BOOKS ABOUT CARING:

Lily's Crossing by Patricia Reilly Giff: published by Yearling, 1999. [Newberry Honor Book]

A Long Way from Chicago by Richard Peck: published by Puffin Books, 2004.

The Secret Garden by Frances Hodgson Burnett: published by Signet Classics, 2003.

Knee-Knock Rise by Natalie Babbitt: published by Square Fish, 2007.

When Hitler Stole Pink Rabbit by Judith Kerr: published by Collins, 2002.

Glossary

Compassion: affected by the suffering of others
Conviction: a strong belief that an idea is right
Empathy: ability to share or "identify with" another person's feelings
Ethics: guidelines about right and wrong
Integrity: knowing and acting on what is right
Persistent: determined not to give up
Stakeholders: people affected by a decision
Universality: applied to everyone

Index

Photo Credits